Finish Yo

[Handwritten inscription: "Felicia! You are a beautiful woman. I think your beauty to the world is already persuasive. Finish Your Book! Finish your book! 3/28/10" with signature]

II Timothy 4:7
I have fought the good fight. I have finished the race. I have kept the faith.

Dr. Michelle R. Loving McKay

Finish Your Course
©2007 by Dr. Michelle R. Loving McKay

Published by MLM Solutions
P.O. Box 105, Holly, MI 48442
Publisher since 2008

Cover Design by
Kreative Power Marketing Solutions

ISBN 978-0-9820766-0-6
ISBN 0-9820766-0-6

Library of Congress Control Number
2008908158

Printed in the United States

Dedication

This book is dedicated to young people and adults who desire to complete their education. It was written with the hope that readers will be motivated and encouraged to keep moving past any obstacles they may encounter. This book is also dedicated to those people who feel they cannot complete their education due to a time lapse or circumstances that seem impossible to beat. Your desire to complete your education can be realized if you first believe in yourself and believe in God's ability to sustain you.

Table of Contents

1   Faith/God: ...15
Hebrews 11:1 reminds us that faith is the substance of things hoped for, the evidence of things not seen.

2   Prayer/Trust: ...23
James 5:16 tells me that the earnest (heartfelt, continued) prayer of a righteous man makes tremendous power available (dynamic in its working).

3   Will/Holy Spirit: ...33
Zechariah 4:6 indicates that it is not by might, nor by power, but by My spirit, saith the Lord of hosts.

4   Jesus Love/Family Support: ...40
Romans 8:35 states that Who shall separate us from the love of Christ?

5   Vision/Desire: ...48
Habakkuk 2:2 says and the Lord answered me and said Write the vision and engrave it so plainly upon tablets that everyone who passes may read as he hastens by.

6 Provision/Finances: ...56
Ecclesiastes 7:12 tells us that wisdom is a defense even as money is a defense, but the excellency of knowledge is that wisdom shields and preserves the life of him who has it.

7 Order/Planning: ...65
Psalms 37:23 reveals that the steps of a good man are ordered by the Lord; and he delighteth in his way.

8 Courage/Persistence: ...73
Joshua 1:7 reminds us only you be strong and very courageous, that you may do according to all the law which Moses My servant commanded you. Turn not from it to the right hand or to the left that you may prosper wherever you go.

9 Commitment/Works: ...84
James 2:20 asks Are you willing to be shown, you foolish fellow, that faith apart from works is inactive and ineffective and worthless?

10 Wisdom/Godly Counsel: ...91
Proverbs 11:14 admonishes that where no counsel is, the people fall: but in the multitude of counselors there is safety.

And Jabez called on the God of Israel in 1 Chronicles 4:10, saying, "Oh that You would bless me and enlarge my border, and that Your hand might be with me, and You would keep me from evil so it might not hurt me! And God granted his request.

Hebrews 13:21 says to strengthen and make you what you ought to be and equip you with everything good that you may carry out His will; works in you and accomplishes that which is pleasing in His sight, through Jesus Christ; to Whom be the glory forever and ever. Amen.

Keep the charge of the Lord your God, walk in His ways, keep His statutes, His commandments, His precepts, and His testimonies, as it is written in the Law of Moses, that you may do wisely and prosper in all that you do and wherever you turn according to 1 Kings 2:3.

Jeremiah 29:11 says For I know the thoughts and plans that I have for you, says the Lord, thoughts and plans for welfare and peace and not for evil, to give you hope in your final outcome.

You will show me the path of life; in Your presence is fullness of joy, at Your right hand, there are pleasures forevermore according to Psalms 16:11.

About the Author

Dr. Michelle R. Loving McKay is a native of Flint, MI and completed her education in the Flint Community Schools. She attended Spelman College in Atlanta, GA and obtained her Bachelor's Degree with a major in Psychology and a minor in Management from Western Michigan University in Kalamazoo, MI. Further education includes a Masters' Degree in Public Administration and a Doctorate of Education from Wayne State University. Her Professional career has included college admissions for 12 years, various corporate and philanthropic work along with Christian service to Decolores and Incarcerated Youth Ministries. She attended Bible Study Fellowship and has a certificate from Word of Life Bible Institute. Dr. Loving McKay has two wonderful children and resides in Michigan. She is a lifelong learner, an avid reader, loves to travel and is a woman devoted to family and friends.

Acknowledgements

It is important to acknowledge those persons that have kept me on course and believed in me when I did not believe in myself. My mother, Pamela Y. Loving has always been my favorite cheerleader. She has encouraged me, supported me, listened to me and been with me through all my ups and downs. My dad, William Copeland must be recognized for being the best Dad in the world. He has also listened and believed in me. I would like to also acknowledge my children; Lauren and Marcus. They have listened to all my lectures on education and trusted me to guide them to a life with God. I would also like to thank Jeanetta for giving me the title for my book while sitting together at a Decolores Ministries workshop and Michelle for her editing contributions. Finally, I must acknowledge my friend Cynthia, who helped me to Dare to Dream by providing her inspirational writing workshops. I did not think anyone would care to hear about my story, however, once the gift was stirred up in me, I was ready to soar. I plan to write other books to encourage and support people through this journey we call life.

10 Important Lessons for the Graduate

1. Make sure to study first, you can have fun later and you will enjoy it more.

2. Develop your relationship with God; you will need to rely on it. Join a Church if you can, either way, pray daily and read the bible and other inspirational books regularly as a guide for your life.

3. Don't be afraid to meet new people and try new things, as long as they are good for you.

4. Stay away from alcohol, drugs and cigarettes, they are addictive and can lead to health problems later and distractions from school now.

5. Eat right, get your rest and stay physically fit.

6. Girlfriends and boyfriends are nice, and friends are fine to have, but do not let them distract you from studying and completing your education first.

7. Study at least 2-3 hours for every 1 hour you are in class. Even though you may only have 12-17 credit hours – you can never over study.

8. Don't be too hard on yourself the first year. Develop a routine that works for you and produces good results.

9. Don't quit, keep your eye on the prize, graduation. Seek help from others when you need it. Find ways to help yourself – financially and or mentally.

10. Keep in touch with your family and friends. You will need them and they need and love you.

You can finish your course!!

Section 1: Spiritual Applications

The pursuit of an education is a major decision that requires thought, planning and determination. There are many spiritual applications that one must apply for the journey to be a successful one. The following chapters listed in this section immediately come to mind. They can be of significant help to you during the entire educational completion process. The educational process is a practical journey, but more importantly a spiritual journey as well. The ability to complete my bachelor's, master's and doctoral degrees would have been impossible without the following spiritual considerations.

Chapter 1: Faith/God

Hebrews 11:1 reminds us that faith is the substance of things hoped for, the evidence of things not seen.

Hebrews 11:1 reminds us that faith is the substance of things hoped for, the evidence of things not seen. A high level of faith is needed to even begin the educational journey. Questions such as how will I pay? Who will pay? Who will accept me into their school? Can I pass the entrance exam? Can I pass the class? Will I be able to make it to all the classes? What about my family? What about work? How long will it take?

We can hope for positive answers to these questions, but not see the outcome or know if it will all work out. In fact, one can get stuck in trying to answer these questions for years before ever applying to any college.

Even though the answers to these questions were not clear to me, I decided to still pursue my dream of a doctoral degree. My bachelor's and master's degree programs were already successfully completed in 1984 and 1992 respectively.

I made a decision to contact schools and complete applications. I took the GRE, a test needed for entrance to graduate school and looked for money to pay for my education. Although acceptance was not granted by any college as of yet, 2 Corinthians 5:7 states that we walk by faith and not by sight. We cannot be moved by what we see or don't see. I had to forge ahead into the unknown in order to create the possibility of beginning and finishing school.

A denial letter from several schools did not stop me

nor should it stop you from pursuing your dream. The school does not really know your capability or you; a negative answer should not define you or your ability. A low-test score on the GRE/ACT/SAT (college entrance exams) or even a lack of understanding the questions on these tests should not stop you from pursuing your dream. You can always take a test preparation workshop to assist your understanding of these exams. Moving forward on the education completion journey is not an option, it is a requirement. The road to completion might be long, but nonetheless forward movement must take place.

After my program was completed, I was able to say like Philippians 3:14, I press on toward the goal to win the (supreme and heavenly) prize to which God in Christ

Jesus is calling us upward. Did I get discouraged? Yes. Did I know how it was all going to come together? No. Did I quit in the midst of difficult times, pressure or confusion in my life? No. Our faith must push us past our circumstances. Faith has to be the driving force used to keep us going even when a lack of clarity or understanding appears to dominate our thinking. Logic must not rule the decisions or steps necessary for future progress. A faith in God must be what moves us and what allows us to believe in what we cannot see.

Genesis 15:6 states and he, Abram believed in (trusted in, relied on, and remained steadfast to) the Lord and He counted it to him as righteousness (right standing with God). I wanted to be in right standing with God. My faith increases my relationship with God because when we trust Him, He will answer. But without faith it is impossible to please and be satisfactory to Him. For whoever would come near to God must believe that God exists and that He is the rewarder of those who earnestly and diligently seek Him out according to Hebrews 11:6.

Faith is something you do—Faith is something you become—you become in right standing with God. You walk in it, you believe. My faith was in an ability to begin, remain and finish school. I fought the fight, I finished the course, and I kept the faith like II Timothy 4:7 reminds us to do and I give all the Glory to God!!

Spiritual applications for Faith

1. Faith is the evidence of things hoped for and not seen
2. We walk by faith and not by sight
3. I have fought a good fight, I have finished the course, I kept the faith
4. I want to be in right standing with God
5. Without faith it is impossible to please God
6. I press on toward the goal to win the prize

Faith Affirmation

My faith is given to me by God. My ability to believe in God's word will give me the strength I need to conquer any obstacle. I trust that God will overcome any fear I have of success. I know that I have the ability in Christ to push pass my self imposed limitations. I speak victory over every class that I must take and I speak understanding to every encounter I must face. I speak understanding to my mind when I am confused about what to do next. I do not fear the unknown for faith is the substance of things hoped for and the evidence of things not seen. I believe that I will finish my education and in that completion, God will be glorified.

Write your own Faith affirmation/goals

_____

_____

_____

_____

_____

_____

_____

_____

_____

_____

_____

_____

_____

Chapter 2: Prayer/Trust

James 5:16 tells me that the earnest (heartfelt, continued) prayer of a righteous man makes tremendous power available (dynamic in its working).

I have often quoted to others that prayer was central to every success and every action that was taken throughout my schooling. It was definitely a challenge for me to get into the Public Administration Master's Degree program at Wayne State University. I scheduled a meeting with the chair of the Public Administration Department due to the denial letter that I received for admittance to the program. I took my portfolio, boldness, faith and prayer right in those doors with me.

The chair decided to grant me entrance in the program on a conditional/provisional basis. This meant a

B grade or better had to be obtained in order to take the next class and be given regular admissions into the program. It was important to meet with the chair to gain admittance. It would have been impossible to move forward if I accepted the denial letter without pursuing other options that were available for admissions. You may have to consider this approach if you are not granted admissions to the university of your choice. You may also have to start out at a community college or your second or third choice of colleges if you don't qualify for admissions initially.

The first public administration course was really a class to determine who would remain in the program. It was a comprehensive course that covered the major tenets of public administration. I was a psychology major and business management minor trying to enter a Public Administration program. It sounded as if the teacher was speaking in a foreign language on the first night of class. My history of public administration was limited and so was my understanding of the major and concepts.

On the way back to my car that night after class, believe it or not, I felt really stupid. Tears came to my eyes and at that very moment it was clear that only prayer, study and hard work would get me through that class. My Prayers were for wisdom, understanding, favor and the ability to comprehend what was being taught. It is with great pride and humility that I note the first difficult class was passed with a B grade. I finished the program with a Master's Degree in Public Administration.

You see James 5:16 tells me that the earnest (heartfelt, continued) prayer of a righteous man makes tremendous power available (dynamic in its working). It was necessary to continuously pray that God would move on my behalf. My master's program was paid for through a company tuition reimbursement program. My doctoral program also required a great amount of prayer. I said "Lord, You have given me desire and confidence in Your ability to pay for this degree. It is possible to be paid for without taking out a loan or money from my family." My prayers and trust in God provided me with the full $30,000+ needed to pay for my doctoral education.

Philippians 4:6 reminds me to be careful for nothing; but in every thing by prayer and supplication with thanksgiving let your requests be made known to God.

There were times when I did not know what to do next. There were times when writer's block was present and just times when my mind, body and emotions were confused, tired or just stuck. Prayer allowed me to hear the Lord say: Have not I commanded you? Be strong, vigorous, and very courageous. Be not afraid, neither be dismayed for the Lord your God is with you wherever you go - Joshua 1:9. He was with me in my meetings, travels, classes, during all my exams, during my dissertation writing and during my defense for the doctoral program.

Prayer changes things. We are told to pray without ceasing. Prayer helped me in the final hour when it wasn't clear if I had completed everything the day before my defense. The records department contacted me and indicated that my transcript could be short of some classes. Prayer helped me to know who to call and where to get answers. My fellow classmate, Patricia, gave me information that helped me during that time. I spoke with professors, class mates, the registrar's office and anyone else that was willing to listen. Prayer was my first step and it works every time.

The defense is a public meeting where you defend the dissertation you have prepared. In my case, this included a 143 page paper. Prayer kept me humble and rewarded me with grace. Wherefore he saith God resisteth the proud but gives grace to the humble-James 4:6. God answered every one of my prayers and He was faithful to me. Deuteronomy 7:9 says know, recognize, and understand therefore that the Lord your God, He is

God, the faithful God, Who keeps covenant and steadfast love and mercy with those who love Him and keep His commandments, to a thousand generations.

Spiritual applications for Prayer/Trust

1. The earnest prayers of a righteous man make tremendous power
2. Be strong, vigorous and very courageous
3. Be not afraid for the Lord your God is with you
4. God resists the proud, but gives grace to the humble
5. Know, recognize, understand that the Lord your God is faithful

Prayer/Trust Affirmation

The prayers of a righteous man availeth much. My prayer time is important. My prayer time draws me closer to God. My prayers allow me to commune with God on a level that feeds my soul. My prayer time is the food and drink I need to make it throughout this educational process and throughout my life. I will pray when I am discouraged, when I don't understand and when I am confused about what to do next. I am a prayer warrior in the good times and the bad. I pray when I feel slighted, when I feel I don't belong or when I am too tired to get out of bed.

I pray for my school, my fellow students, for my professors and for my increase in knowledge. I pray for my family, my children and my friends. I pray for my health, my mind and my strength. I pray for this nation. I pray that my purpose be fulfilled. I pray that I will complete my education in a timely manner and that I will have all I need to graduate at the top of my class. I pray that the Holy Spirit will guide me and that I will have favor with God and man. I pray that my new business or career opportunity is waiting for me and I will be ready for it when purpose and destiny meet.

Write your own Prayer/Trust affirmation/goals

_____

_____

_____

_____

_____

_____

_____

_____

_____

_____

_____

_____

_____

Chapter 3: Will/Holy Spirit

Zechariah 4:6 indicates that it is not by might, nor by power, but by My spirit, saith the Lord of hosts.

The Spirit of the Lord was with me and I was confident that I would finish the doctoral program. [Besides this evidence] it was also established and plainly endorsed by God, Who showed His approval of it by signs and wonders (my acceptance into a doctoral program close to home; my $20,000 scholarship being approved before I was fully accepted plus $10,000 more that was needed later) and various miraculous manifestations (my promotion at work freeing my time to take classes, my family support) of [His] power— Hebrews 2:4 and by imparting the gifts of the Holy Spirit [to the believers] according to His own will.

My belief that God was with me and that He would help me complete the doctoral program is supported by Zechariah 4:6 which tells me that it is not by might, nor by power, but by My spirit, saith the Lord of hosts. The beginning days of the doctoral process are like yesterday. It was important to have a Chair for my committee. The Chair serves a very important role and gives much of their time, energy and dedication to the journey. I met with a potential chair that authored several books and was very impressive; however, she said that she never had a student finish the doctoral process. She also was somewhat discouraging because it appeared that she did not believe in my abilities or the opportunities that were available to me in the program. She said my lack of an education background would hinder me and that it would be difficult to be accepted. She really did not want to be my Chair. I understood that and did not let her words become life to me or take root in my spirit.

Beloved, do not put faith in every spirit, but prove (test) the spirits to discover whether they proceed from God; for many false prophets have gone forth into the world - 1 John 4:1. Although, I don't know whether or not she was a real prophet, I know that what she was prophesying was not part of my future. Not in your own strength, for it is God Who is all the while effectually at work in you energizing and creating in you the power and desire, both to will and to work for His good pleasure and satisfaction and delight- Philippians 2:13.

What if I had believed what she said? What if I decided to end my pursuit of a chair or completion of the program based on her comments? What if I had let a spirit of rejection come on me because she did not want to be my Chair? I would be letting the wrong voice dictate my future.

When he has brought his own sheep outside, he walks on before them, and the sheep follow him because they know his voice. They will never [on any account] follow a stranger, but will run away from him because they do not know the voice of strangers or recognize their call-St. John 10:4-5. I was glad to know my Father's voice at that time so that I would only follow His voice.

Spiritual applications for Will/Holy Spirit

1. Plainly endorsed by God who showed His approval
2. Not by might, nor by power, but by His Spirit
3. Do not put faith in every spirit, but test the spirit
4. Not in your own strength, but God's
5. The sheep follow him because they know His voice
6. The voice of a stranger they will not follow

Will/Holy Spirit Affirmation

The Holy Spirit guides me. The Holy Spirit is my counselor and my comforter. The Holy Spirit instructs me on what to do and not do and even on what to say or not say. I am directed on how to choose my school and my classes by the Holy Spirit. I seek the counsel of the Holy Spirit before I make any decisions. I am in tune with the Holy Spirit and I am not alone in any of my decision making processes. The Holy Spirit attracts the right relationships to me and removes the relationships that may be detrimental to my life and my career opportunities. I am drawn by the Holy Spirit and confirmation comes to me before I decide to make a bad decision. The Holy Spirit will counsel me and I will listen.

Write your own Will/Holy Spirit affirmation/goals

_____

_____

_____

_____

_____

_____

_____

_____

_____

_____

_____

_____

_____

Chapter 4: Jesus Love/Family Support

Romans 8:35 states that Who shall separate us from the love of Christ?

For God so loved the world that He gave His only begotten Son, that whosoever believeth in Him should not perish, but have everlasting life - John 3:16. What love God has for us, in that while we were still sinners, Christ died for us. Many obstacles come to my mind when it comes to education and they sound a lot like those mentioned in Romans 8:35…

- Suffering
- Affliction
- Tribulation
- Calamity
- Distress
- Persecution
- Hunger
- Destitution
- Peril
- Sword

Romans 8:35-39 states that Who shall separate us from the love of Christ? Shall suffering and affliction and tribulation? Or calamity and distress? Or persecution or hunger or destitution or peril, or sword? As it is written, for Thy sake we are killed all the day long; we are accounted as sheep for the slaughter. Yet amid all these things we are more than conquerors and gain a surpassing victory through Him Who loved us. For I am persuaded beyond doubt (am sure), that neither death, nor life, nor angels, nor principalities, nor powers, nor things impending and threatening nor things to come, nor powers, nor height, nor depth, nor anything else in all creation will be able to separate us from the love of God, which is in Christ Jesus our Lord.

What do you do when one or more of the above areas

come your way? What if you are in school? Do you quit? Do you rearrange and adjust your schedule? Do you stop and perhaps start back later? Do you stop and never start back again? Life happens. We will encounter some difficulties. It is important to learn that throughout any educational program that family support is critical. Sometimes it is not perfect. Sometimes you can not study at the most convenient times and you have to squeeze study time in during the wee hours of the morning.

It was a challenge to begin my doctoral program initially since my children were three and seven years old. Support is necessary when it comes to caring for young children. My class schedule included classes two days a week for 2 ½ years in the winter, fall and spring.

42

A 12 hour comprehensive exam was also required for my doctoral program and intense study helped me pass the exam successfully. An eight hour comprehensive exam was also necessary for the masters program. In addition for doctoral completion, I had to finish my dissertation which was a 143 page document that included many meetings with my Chair and my committee, along with consultation work that enhanced my ability to fine tune my statistical data.

My family helped take care of my children's needs when I had class or work. You can get a babysitter or family member to assist you with child care needs if you are single. My children were also supportive. They did not once ask me to quit school or make me feel guilty for completing my education. We would have plenty of quality time together. My son would often wait up for me during the evening hours to tell me good night and have me tuck him in bed. Those were very special times for me.

It was my hope that they would gain some educational fortitude from seeing me in school and that by watching me, a transfer of commitment would occur towards their own education. My 12 year old daughter and my immediate family were able to sit in with me when my dissertation was presented. My extended family was able to attend the ceremony and celebrate dinner with me during my doctoral degree graduation in May of 2006. My parents also supported me during the pursuit of my education. Friends and extended family also encouraged me during my educational journey.

Spiritual applications for Jesus Love/Family Support

1. Nothing can separate us from the love of God
2. God will not leave us or forsake us
3. He has sent a comforter to support us in our time of need
4. For God so loved the world that He gave His only begotten Son

Jesus Love/ Family Affirmations

The Lord is the center of my being. He died on the cross because He loves me and wants what is best for me. I am confident that as I trust in Him, all the needs of my family will be met. The love of Christ allows me freedom to express my love to others in a way that strengthens the entire family. My family flows in peace and harmony while I am in school. There are no obstacles or weapons that will be formed against my family while I am in school. I know that I am connected to the true vine of

45

Christ which gives me the life I need to nourish myself and my family with the love we need. I have the ability to love all those God puts in my life. My love permeates every class, every professor and every fellow student. The love I receive after I have fellowshipped with God's word will allow me to freely love those in my family with the perfect love of Christ.

Write your own Jesus Love/Family affirmation/goals

_____

_____

_____

_____

_____

_____

_____

_____

_____

_____

_____

_____

_____

Chapter 5: Vision/Desire

Habakkuk 2:2 says and the Lord answered me and said Write the vision and engrave it so plainly upon tablets that everyone who passes may read as he hastens by.

Once vision has been birthed, desire will follow. It became apparent to me when I was pursuing my bachelors degree that education would always be a part of my life. Vision helps birth purpose. Habakkuk 2:2-3 states and the Lord answered me and said, Write the vision and engrave it so plainly upon tablets that everyone who passes may read as he hastens by. For the vision is for an appointed time and it hastens to the end; it will not deceive or disappoint. Though it tarry, wait for it, because it will surely come; it will not be behindhand on its appointed day.

College was always a part of my future. My grandfather, Dr. Alvin D. Loving, Sr. received his doctoral degree in 1956 and helped guide all his grandchildren to a path of education. We all knew we would get an education. My grandfather used to say "No one can take your education away from you." He would quote our family motto: "Good, Better, Best, never let it rest until your good is better and your better, best."

It was evident to me during my senior year in high school that Spelman College in Atlanta was my first and only college of choice. Spelman accepted me and thank God they did, since it was the only college application I completed. Graduating from high school with honors helped me gain acceptance. Spelman provided great opportunities and it was so exciting to be at an all girls black college. There were great professors and great roommates.

The opportunity to live in Atlanta, GA was more than one could imagine. I explored Atlanta and met people from all over the country. There were great seminars to attend, awesome speakers like Julian Bond and Stokely Carmichael, just to name a few. However, shortly after my first semester, I became homesick and my mother was ill, so transferring to Western Michigan University after my first semester sophomore year seemed to be the best option at that time.

My bachelor's degree in Psychology was completed after 2 ½ years at Western. It is fine to transfer to another college if a change is necessary due to unforeseeable events. Students transfer all the time due to finances, majors offered, family issues, etc. My grandfather, great uncle, and two aunts attended Western. My brother was also a student at Western so my living opportunity was immediate. I moved in with him and his roommate in January. It was like the old sitcom, Three's Company. However, I was the only female. It was great fun living with my brother and it provided instant access to friends.

Five years later, after graduating from Western Michigan, I began work on my Masters degree in Public Administration at Wayne State University. My application was denied initially. However, after encouraging myself, as I indicated earlier, I decided to meet with the Chair of the department with a prepared portfolio of all my achievements and he admitted me on a provisional basis. I was granted admissions after passing the provisional class and completed my masters program three years later. It was 10 years afterward when I began work on my doctoral program in Education: Curriculum and Instruction-K -12 education.

My doctoral program was completed in March of 2006 while working and the mother of two school-aged children. Vision helps propel a future. Vision helps birth desire. Desire fulfilled, creates action that moves one toward a dream. My path was not perfectly smooth. There were several jobs and relocations, some failed relationships and family losses during my educational journey. However, vision will cause you to keep moving and living a life destined for purpose. Remember that time is always passing and you can take a class or learn something each day to move you closer to completion.

Spiritual applications for Vision/Desire:

1. Without vision, people perish
2. With vision, comes provision
3. Desire can lead to motivation
4. God's plans for us are to give us a hope and a future

Vision/Desire Affirmations:

God gives me the desire to have a perfect vision for my life. I know that without a vision, I will perish. I am called to achieve great things because the plans God has for me are for a hope and future and to prosper me. My desires line up perfectly with the will of God and I will fulfill the call He has on my life. I can do all things through Christ that strengthens me. My steps are ordered of God. I will quiet myself so that my ear will be inclined to hear and my eyes will be inclined to see what God has in store for me. I put total trust in the Lord as He reveals

His will and purpose in my life. I will gain clarity from the Lord as I seek first His kingdom and then all other things will be added unto me.

Write your own Vision/Desire affirmation/goals

Chapter 6: Provision/Finances

Ecclesiastes 7:12 tells us that wisdom is a defense even as money is a defense, but the excellency of knowledge is that wisdom shields and preserves the life of him who has it.

Provision for your education completion is important to make sure you can pay all your college expenses. How can you expect to pay for an education if you don't have the money? School is expensive and it is not getting any cheaper. I had the vision for my education and the desire; however, financing my education was still unclear. Even though the money was not available, the vision was not derailed or stopped just because the money question wasn't solved. I began a series of conversations about options for paying for education.

Mary Ann, a friend of mine does this whenever she

has a need. For instance, she needed a riding lawn mower. She began talking about it to everyone around her. She asked her co-workers. She asked her neighbors, friends, and even strangers. Eventually, the riding lawn mower materialized. However, she also needed the money to pay for it, so she began asking for that as well and the money appeared. We have not because we ask not. We must be willing to ask for what we need so that we can draw that item, the money or the people we need to us.

People began sharing with me and the favor of God and man drew near to me. I was told about fellowships and scholarships that could help pay for my education. God blessed me with a $20,000 fellowship and an additional $10,000 which helped cover the cost of my entire doctoral program. The approval of the money for the initial $20,000 fellowship occurred before acceptance was fully granted to the college.

Michelle, a friend of mine helped me with obtaining the additional $10,000 needed. I contacted a colleague about additional funding and he did not contact me right away so I was going to forget about it. However, she encouraged me and said maybe he is busy or didn't get the message so perhaps you should call again. I called him back.

I did not want to become a pest or bother him, and maybe pride got in the way. However, she said the only way you can obtain the money is by calling and asking, and that is exactly what was needed. He told me he was busy and unable to follow up with me right away, however, the additional funding was available for me. Matt 7:7 reminds me to ask and it will be given to me. This was surely the hand of God.

Provision and finances can either help or hinder your schooling opportunity or catapult you along the way. Tuition reimbursement was also provided for my master's program. This is an important area to consider when selecting a job after you complete your bachelor's degree. Some employers will provide tuition reimbursement as a benefit of employment. You should be sure and research the company to see if this educational development opportunity is available to you.

You have to keep moving forward in your conversations about covering your college expenses. Psalms 1:3 indicates that you shall be like a tree planted by the rivers of water, that brings forth fruit in your season; your leaf shall not wither; and whatsoever you do shall prosper.

The internet along with other avenues is a great place to research scholarship and fellowship opportunities. Also co-workers and college graduates can give you helpful advice about funding your college education. You should not stop pursuing your dream of obtaining a college education just because you don't know how you are going to pay for it.

There is a law of attraction at work in you. How you think and what you spend time pursing and thinking about will help enable you and thrust you into a world of provision that you never thought was available. You can work on college campuses or work a regular job and even get financial aid to pay for college. What you can not afford to do is say you don't have the money and you don't know how you are going to pay for it. You can not wait until the money comes because in your action toward your education, you will discover a new realm of opportunity that is only available to those who pursue their dreams.

Spiritual applications for Provision/Finances

1. God will supply all your needs according to His riches in glory
2. You have not, because you ask not
3. You must have vision in order to receive provision
4. You must first believe in order to receive and achieve

Provision/Finance affirmations

I attract everything that I need by what I say and the actions that I take. Everything that I have need of is available to me if I just ask. Ask and it will be given unto me; seek and I shall find; knock and the door will be opened unto to me. For when I ask I receive; when I seek I find; and when I knock, the door will be opened (Matt 7:7-8). I am not afraid of provision. Money cometh to me and I am a magnet to receive all that I have need of during this time of educational pursuit. I meet the right people and I have the right conversations that will ensure that my education is fully paid for with money left over. All my classes are paid for in full and my books and fees are fully funded. Any child care I need is handled. Any obstacle that comes my way financially is fully covered. I am wealthy and rich in my thinking. No weapon formed against me shall prosper (Isa 54:17). The joy of the Lord is my strength (Ne 8:10).

Write your own Provision/Finances affirmation/goals

_____

_____

_____

_____

_____

_____

_____

_____

_____

_____

_____

_____

_____

Chapter 7: Order/Planning

Psalms 37:23 reveals that the steps of a good man are ordered by the Lord; and he delighteth in his way.

Planning when to pursue your education is going to make a big difference in your ability to complete it. Timing will always manifest itself in our life. It can work in our favor by supporting our ability to be a success or a failure in the results we desire to produce. Order in my life will display itself in my timeliness, presentation, preparation and in how my life is portrayed. Confusion is present when order is absent.

Order will allow me to plan and succeed in the areas of my life that are most central to my peace. Order and planning go hand in hand. I can not plan if I don't have order. It doesn't have to mean that your life is perfectly set up and that your towels are folded flawlessly and your floor is sparkling. It doesn't even have to mean that all your purses, shoes and outfits are coordinated on a daily basis. What it does mean to me is that your life is in order such that the plans you have can come to pass in a relatively uncomplicated and peaceful manner.

This is even true for the college planning process. You may lose your spot at the school you are planning to attend if you don't select the school you would like to go to early in the process. Many parents and students are disappointed when they contact schools to get in after the deadline has passed and the waitlist process has started. Many students are disappointed when they don't have the grades they need to get into the school of their choice.

Both of these examples lend themselves to a lack of order and a lack of planning. In the first example, the student could have been prepared to apply to their top choices for college. The student could have looked online or visited colleges during the freshman, sophomore or junior year in high school as part of the early exploration process.

There is a plan to follow during college exploration and an order that can help you secure your space at the college of your choice. A timely review prepares you to apply to your top choices for college in early fall of the senior year. It is best to figure out where to attend near the beginning of the process since colleges provide so many opportunities for you to learn about what is available.

Acceptance is just the first step toward enrollment in the college of your choice. The next steps after acceptance include financial aid, scholarship application, along with housing and orientation deposits depending upon college requirements. Colleges typically determine who will be attending based on students completing these common steps.

The second example involves an academically under prepared student unqualified to get admitted to the college of their choice. This student could have taken the right courses, planned to meet with tutors for difficult classes, completed homework and studied for upcoming tests. However, the poor planning of this student will not allow them to get into the school of their choice.

A presence of order in their life would have led

them to pick the right classes, select tutors, get off the telephone and complete homework and establish regular study times. Order and planning produce the results needed to be successful in college.

My planning to complete school before my kids were busy with sports and other activities was done on purpose. I knew that it would be difficult to complete my schooling while they were in their middle years so the plan was to complete school during their early years.

My life was ordered in a way so study time could occur while they were sleeping. Although there were some evening classes, quality time made it possible to spend time with them and tuck them in bed after evening classes. The Lord will help you to know when the best time for school is for you and He will give you the plan and create an order that will allow you to be successful.

Spiritual applications for Order/Planning

1. The steps of a righteous man are ordered of God
2. God is a God of order
3. God is not the author of any chaos or confusion
4. Harmony and peace should exist in my mind before order can occur in my life

Order/Planning Affirmation

I plan my life for success. My steps are ordered from God. My life demonstrates order in every area. I am on time to all my appointments and my classes. I get all of my papers and assignments in on time. I study in a quiet space and prepare fully for every class. I exceed in every class because my work is excellent and I am skilled at listening. I pay attention so that I know when my assignments are due and what is expected of me. I do not get upset or critical of myself when my plans do not succeed. I create a new plan to get all my work done in a way that meets my goals. I do not neglect my family, however, I balance my schedule so that I can get the most out of my day. I get help with my plan if it seems that it is not working for me. I am not afraid to change the order as long as it keeps me in the game. I do not quit even when it gets tough. I keep my life in order and my plan in tact when many obstacles would try to hinder me from reaching my dream of completing my education.

Write your own Order/Planning affirmation/goals

_____

_____

_____

_____

_____

_____

_____

_____

_____

_____

_____

_____

_____

_____

Chapter 8: Courage/Persistence

Joshua 1:7 reminds us only you be strong and very courageous, that you may do according to all the law which Moses My servant commanded you. Turn not from it to the right hand or to the left that you may prosper wherever you go.

According to Webster's dictionary courage means mental or moral strength to venture, persevere, and withstand danger, fear, or difficulty. It takes courage to pursue an education. You may be the first one in your family to get a degree. You may not even know what steps to take to complete your admissions application or obtain financial aid. Your ability to understand the language that is used by college personnel may even be lacking. However, your courage can kick in and help you to have strength to venture and overcome any difficulty or challenge that may come your way. Fear can stop you from moving forward.

The thought of a college setting may seem overwhelming because the environment does not reflect what you have previously experienced at your high school or in your home environment. Your courage will allow you to withstand any obstacle. It took courage for me to continue my education. My career path was not solidified; however, it was certain that my bachelor's degree in Psychology would not be enough to sustain me financially. It was important to continue educationally. I can recall wanting to go out of state to college during my high school years.

My high school was predominantly white and my desire was to see what it would be like to attend a historically black college. My application was accepted at Spelman College. At that time, I had no clue as to how my college would be paid for and did not think about the expense that it would be to my mother. A persistent attitude will keep you moving forward to meet your dreams even though that may mean you have a selfish attitude towards the people you love.

My mother was determined to help me reach my dream, so she cashed in her stocks to make my hope of attending Spelman a reality. She did not want me looking back later in life on that experience in a negative way. She did not want anything to stop me from moving forward and reaching any of my dreams. She and my dad supported my education and my decision to attend Spelman financially and emotionally.

It was a difficult first year. There was so much excitement about leaving home; however, the wanting to return home was met equally with great anticipation. It was adventurous to be away from home and experience all the excitement and exposure to African American leadership. It seems that you can only typically gain this dominant leadership experience at a black institution. Even though I had this experience, I was ready to leave after the first year because I was homesick and my mother became ill.

My curiosity and new friends encouraged me to stay another semester, but eventually a transfer to Western Michigan University was eminent since it was a school closer to home. The transfer was scary because it was mid-year and it was hard to know what to expect.

My transfer to Western Michigan University involved finding a place to stay, so luckily, my brother and his roommate had an extra room for me. It was necessary to adjust to a new environment and meet many new people.

Great opportunity allowed me to work several jobs on campus, pledge Delta Sigma Theta Sorority and graduate 2 ½ years later. The transfer proved to be the best decision for me. It may be necessary for you to transfer if it means you will finish college and be in an environment conducive to your success. It took courage to transfer and it also took courage to believe in myself and finish college in a timely manner.

Several years later I sought information out from a few schools to determine which program to pursue for my master's program. Law school was considered, along with business school and public administration. Public Administration seemed to be the best fit for me at the time since the United Way was my employer and I had always been committed to public service. My courage had to kick in when my initial admissions application to Wayne State was rejected, however, admissions was eventually granted. Sometime later, the doctoral program was pursued and I was denied admissions to a couple of schools during that process as well. Psychology and political science were considered. However, because education was always interesting to me and an area of enjoyment, I enrolled in Wayne State's Education Curriculum and Instruction program and was accepted. It was inconclusive as to how my education would be paid for; however, there remained a great confidence in my belief that completion was inevitable. The interview process and request for funding was successful. It was a dream that had finally come true.

A dissertation is a necessary component for completing a doctoral studies program. Your research adds relevant information to the body of knowledge on that specific topic. The dissertation consists of a topic that you select and develop through research, statistical data, and population study along with report conclusion.

Research for the dissertation can be gathered throughout the process if the topic is already selected. Initially I had an 18 page bibliography. The majority of the writing and organizing for the dissertation was worked on after completing my course work. Completing the dissertation took all the courage I could muster up because the process is totally self- propelled.

You have to follow all the steps in order to complete your dissertation according to the format required by the university. You must be persistent, unrelenting, unwavering and completely focused in order to finish the program. Nothing can stand in your way. Webster's dictionary defines persistence as continuing to exist in spite of interference or treatment.

It was important to continue to persist with my requirements for graduation although my life was full with a family and a job. My life also included active church participation and service to Decolores Ministries and Incarcerated Youth Ministries. School was very central to my life, but so were my family and my relationship with God.

You must persist toward the very end even if your family is in a crisis situation. You must persist in spite of interference in order to complete the school process. You must also persist and have courage in your academic pursuits. However, most importantly, you should always remember that the word of God will sustain you and keep you during every step of the process.

Spiritual applications for Courage/Persistence

1. Be strong and very courageous
2. Don't let the book of the law depart from you, but meditate on it day and night
3. Fight the good fight of faith, finish the race
4. Let no weapon formed against you prosper

Courage/Persistence Affirmation

I can do all things through Christ that gives me strength. I must be courageous and persist even when I don't feel like it. Even if it looks difficult and all the odds are stacked up against me, I can take courage and persist in reaching my goals. My determination is in my ability to believe in myself and to stand in a place of power. Nothing can deter me from moving in the direction of finishing my education. It may storm and a tornado can be going on around me, but my focus is on my completion. I am capable of balancing activities and taking care of the needs of my family. However, I must take time to care for my needs as well. My courage will allow me to connect with the right people and it will allow me to be confident in the areas that are unfamiliar to me. I will succeed. Even when fear tries to rob me of my victory, I will call on courage and wisdom and they will answer me.

Write your own Courage/Persistence

affirmation/goals

_____

_____

_____

_____

_____

_____

_____

_____

_____

_____

_____

_____

Chapter 9: Commitment/Works

James 2:20 asks Are you willing to be shown, you foolish fellow, that faith apart from works is inactive and ineffective and worthless?

Commitment requires that we pledge or commit to do something in the future according to Webster's dictionary. My commitment will determine my success at reaching my goal. I must commit to work toward degree completion. If there is no commitment, it will be impossible to complete my education. There has to be a commitment to the overall completion of my education. That is the major commitment upon which all the others will stand.

There are many papers, exams, group work and homework assignments that are part of the college process. Some of the classes you have to take may not be of interest to you; however, they are required to complete your degree. I remember an accounting class that I had to take for my minor in management during my bachelor's degree program. I was not a numbers person nor did I care about accounting. I had a friend help me with the assignment and my professor discovered that I did not complete the assignment on my own. I received a low grade in that class and it was an important lesson learned.

We have to do our own work in all of our classes unless it is indicated otherwise. We have to put in the time to understand the subject matter even if it is not our favorite class. We learn what we don't like while in college, but we also are empowered to have a level of understanding in a variety of important topics that can help us later. This is one of the values of a liberal arts education.

Once there is commitment to my education, the next steps to completing my schooling will become possible. You have to be committed to registering every semester. Commitment must come when securing funding for your education through financial aid, fellowships or scholarship searches. There may be obstacles that come up during each semester of class; however, you must be committed to getting through the semester. Your car may break down, your relationship may end and you may even bomb on one of your homework assignments. However, you must do the work and stay committed to completing the class so that you can meet the goal of completing your education.

It is not apparent if commitment is taught, learned or ingrained. However, you must grab a hold of commitment and hard work in order to complete your education. I was committed even though a transfer at the undergraduate level occurred in mid year from one school to another with a loss of some credits. Once you commit, you have to be willing to do all the hard work that is required. You will have to stay up late and lose some sleep depending upon the classes and the assignments required. My masters and doctoral program required going the extra mile and not necessarily knowing or understanding everything that was needed to be successful. However, my commitment to education and my commitment to do the work sustained me during the rough times of the educational process.

Spiritual applications for Commitment/Works

1. Faith without works is dead
2. He that does not work does not eat
3. Commit your ways to God
4. God will give us witty inventions and give us the ability to create wealth

Commitment/Work Affirmations

I am committed to completing my education. I will surround myself with people that will assist me in meeting my goal. I will study everyday and be sure to put myself in circumstances that will help me to complete my schooling. I will work with my mind and connect with my teachers even if I don't like them or understand what they are teaching. I will pray for understanding of the subject and commit my thoughts to the class I am taking. I will not be distracted no matter what comes up to try to take me off my course of completion. I plan to finish even if the money is tight, even if I get a poor grade on my exam and even if I feel like I don't understand the material. I will get the necessary help to deal with what ever obstacle comes my way.

Write your own Commitment/Work affirmation/goals

_____

_____

_____

_____

_____

_____

_____

_____

_____

_____

_____

_____

_____

Chapter 10: Wisdom/Godly Counsel

Proverbs 11:14 admonishes that where no counsel is, the people fall: but in the multitude of counselors there is safety.

Wisdom is different from knowledge and intellect. Wisdom means ability to discern inner qualities within people and relationships. It means to have a wise attitude, judgment or course of action. Wisdom can allow you to discern when you should speak and the course of action you should take when dealing with your professors and completing your homework. It will also help you know when to be quiet. Proverbs 4:7 tells us that wisdom is the principal thing; therefore get wisdom: and with all thy getting get understanding. For instance you could have an upcoming test; however, if you study the wrong material, you could flunk the test. You also may need to study with a group to get certain concepts in class. It may mean that studying alone may cost you the A grade you so desperately need. I remember taking several statistic classes during my master's program and realizing that statistics was such a foreign topic for me.

I decided to take advantage of a study group that met weekly instead of trying to figure it out alone. This extra study time with the group helped me to get A's and B's in all my statistic classes at the master's and doctoral level as well.

Wisdom can help you select the program that is right for you. You may be better with people and social programs, yet you decide to pursue a major that is void of dealing with people. Wisdom will cause you to discern what will be best for you based on previous experiences. Wisdom will draw you to the right people. Proverbs 11:14 speaks about the value of having a multitude of counselors. The friends in your life are important as they provide the necessary advice and support to help secure what God has in store for you.

You may be thinking of quitting school or moving to another country. Your ability to pursue Godly counsel can help you with timing and with possible financial support. However, if you operate in isolation, you may miss out on reduced tuition, course books or partnership opportunities that could provide a quality oversees experience.

My Committee Chair for my doctoral program was a pastor and she provided much Godly counsel to me. I asked her questions about my program, but I also spoke with her about personal issues and concerns. She would often help me to relax and admonish me to enjoy the journey and quit focusing on the destination.

She had already gone through the process and helped many others, so wisdom would dictate that she had knowledge, ability and understanding that was good for me. Sometimes if you are a person with a know it all attitude, you can cut off opportunities or learning experiences that could benefit you in the long run. Psalms 111:10 warns me that the fear of the Lord is the beginning of wisdom.

Spiritual applications for Wisdom/Godly Counsel

1. The fear of the Lord is the beginning of wisdom
2. Wisdom is the principal thing
3. Seek Godly counsel
4. Get information from a multitude of counselors

Wisdom/Godly Counsel Affirmations

I will seek wisdom because I understand it is the principal thing. My wisdom will add to my ability to make wise decisions and connect me with Godly counsel. I will search out wisdom while she is calling me. I must gain wisdom in order to complete my education. Wisdom will teach me how to get the proper rest and have the right balance during my educational years. Wisdom will help me pick the right school, program, counselors, major and friends. Wisdom will direct my path when danger is near or when I need to change my direction. Wisdom will guide my decisions regarding relationships and my spare time. My relationships will be perfect for me because wisdom will lead me in my decisions.

Write your own Wisdom/Godly affirmation/goals

_____

_____

_____

_____

_____

_____

_____

_____

_____

_____

_____

_____

_____

Section 2: Practical Applications

Practical steps are those areas that require one to work and accomplish activities that will move you forward in the college completion process. You have to plan and take many action steps for college preparation. Once you decide to attend college, you have to arrange other areas in your life to line up with your decision. I have included basic steps that will be helpful in the beginning stages of your college search process.

Chapter 11: Deciding to Attend College

And Jabez called on the God of Israel in 1 Chronicles 4:10, saying, "Oh that You would bless me and enlarge my border, and that Your hand might be with me, and You would keep me from evil so it might not hurt me!" And God granted his request.

Some of you may be wondering is college for me? Maybe you are the first to attend college in your family. Perhaps you are going because that is the family expectation. Whatever your reason may be, college is a practical and important pathway to choose during this time in our history. There have been different times in history where education was not necessary.

The agriculture and industrial age have both faired well for the uneducated population, however, the technological and information era have required more knowledge and skills needed to perform certain jobs. You definitely need more skills than in previous years for just about everything. The knowledge needed to operate your own telephone; cable and banking system require more skills than in previous years, just to name a few.

Educational paths will lead you in different directions depending upon who you are and where you are in life. The best time to pursue your education is directly after your graduation from high school. Typically you do not have a family to support nor do you have major financial or family responsibilities. In fact, many parents help their children financially and emotionally during this transition time in life. Countless students can even get financial aid based upon meeting certain economic factors. You may be out of high school with family responsibilities and financial obligations. Some of you may even be employed or unemployed. You can still pursue your education if you so desire at any time in your life.

Education opens up your world, your thinking and your opportunities. You are typically paid more based on the problems that you are able to solve. You will have a hard time finding employment if you are not skilled. It is a guarantee that you will compete with many people that have developed more talents than you if you don't gain some education or skill. It is always better to be in a position of strength and power when you are looking for employment. Your decision to attend college can be based on several questions such as: What type of problem do I want to solve? What type of house do I want to live in? Do I want to walk to work or have my own car? Do I want to go on vacation every year or not? Do I want to find the cure for cancer? Do I want health benefits? Do I want to eat on a regular basis? Your education is not restricted to college. You can always learn a trade such as plumbing, cosmetology, construction, etc. However, the purpose of this book is to focus on college as the learning path of choice.

You also have to consider how focused you will be while in college and compare that to how focused you were in high school. Many of the subjects in high school will be presented in college. You may have to take some refresher courses to get your head back in the realm of learning especially if you blew off your high school years. You can be college bound by starting with a few classes or you can jump right in and chart a course for earning your associates, bachelors, masters and yes, even a doctoral degree! Your desire for college along with an action plan will make college completion a reality in your life. Once you have made the decision to attend, you are well on your way to completing your education.

Practical applications for Deciding to Attend College

1. Take a personal inventory of your goals and your dreams. Write them down.
2. Make a list of all your monthly expenses such as house, car, etc. with a monthly cost and multiply it by 12 which will give you a total budget for the year. This can help determine how much it will cost you to live. This list can be actual or desired expenses.
3. Talk with positive friends and family that have gone to college previously.
4. Make the decision to attend college, visit several colleges and meet the application deadline prior to the semester in which you plan to attend.

Deciding to Attend College affirmations

College is for me. I have what it takes. I am excited about my graduation date because I am a finisher. I am talented, gifted and a fast learner. I have big dreams that require training and development. Since I have made the decision to attend college, I have drawn people and financial opportunities to pay for college and support me in my desire to finish in a timely manner. My decision is a good one and will allow me to contribute to my community and to my family. The direction that I am taking to learn more about different subjects will expand my world. It will allow me to express myself better because I will be more knowledgeable. I am confident that everything I need will come my way as I take all the steps to get enrolled in the right college for me. I will contact several colleges to get admissions materials. I will talk with counselors, friends and family so that I am empowered. I will have the best information I need to make the most excellent decision about the college I will attend.

Write your own Attend College affirmation/goals

_____

_____

_____

_____

_____

_____

_____

_____

_____

_____

_____

_____

_____

_____

Chapter 12: Selecting and Applying to a College

Hebrews 13:21 says to strengthen and make you what you ought to be and equip you with everything good that you may carry out His will; works in you and accomplishes that which is pleasing in His sight, through Jesus Christ; to Whom be the glory forever and ever. Amen.

Congratulations on your decision to attend college! Your selection and application process can be a simple one if you prepare and plan at least 1-2 years prior to your first college class. There are many things to consider when selecting a college. Examine yourself by answering the following questions:

1. What type of student have I been in previous learning environments?

2. Do I want to move away from home or stay

close to home?

3. Am I comfortable in small classes or large classes?

4. What type of college can I afford? $2,000 or even $45,000 per year?

5. Can I get an athletic, service or academic scholarship?

6. Have I attended any pre-college programs or taken a college preparatory course load?

7. Am I willing to set up visits to the colleges of my choice?

8. Do I have internet access so I can visit colleges online prior to an actual visit?

9. Do I have a mentor or sufficient help to support my plans for attending college?

10. Am I prepared to be disciplined and focus my time on my college courses?

The above questions are just a sampling of questions to ask yourself prior to selecting the college of your choice. It is important to select a college that fits your character, your personality and your style of learning. Many students transfer and even fail the first year of college due to poor preparation and planning. The first year can be successful if you do your homework and select wisely during the college search process. You can visit the internet and learn about the college before you visit. You can also visit campuses or attend open houses at colleges by contacting the college's admissions office.

College recruiters also visit the high schools and community colleges to speak with prospective students.

High school counselors and college advisors are also invaluable resources for students interested in colleges and scholarship opportunities. There are also college nights that are held at various high schools and other locations to give you more information about local and out of state colleges. Your college search will ensure that you select the college best for you; however, it will require time and effort on your part.

My college search process was different for my undergraduate and graduate programs. It was my desire to attend a historically black college for the first year of college. I only applied to Spelman College in Atlanta, GA and fortunately my acceptance was immediate. However, you should not limit your application process to one school. It is important to apply to at least three colleges to increase your options in case changes occur with your life.

The graduate selection process was different due to my life circumstances. I was settled in one city and working. My decision to attend Wayne State University at the master's level and at the doctoral level was due to the quality programs, convenience and program offerings. However, my research was still intense and included gathering information from a variety of schools in Michigan by simply calling and requesting an application packet from several schools.

Once you have selected your college, you must begin the application process. This process can seem over-whelming; however, if you generate all the applicant information on a separate sheet of paper you can transfer it to multiple applications. Most schools generally request the same information. You should note that some schools will require an essay or request additional attachments based on the school and the application packet criteria. You should answer all the questions on the application honestly.

In most cases you will need to pay an application fee and submit transcripts and test scores if you are entering college as an incoming freshman. Transfer students follow a different application routine; however, they also complete an application and request that transcripts be sent from their registrar's office. In some cases, high school transcripts may also be requested.

The application is usually your first introduction to the college so be sure to turn in a thorough and neat application. Also, you should apply at least 1 year or semester before you plan to attend the college of your choice. This will vary based on the college you are selecting, the area you live in and the level of demand from college to college.

Practical applications for Selecting and Applying to College

1. Start your college selection research early.
2. Use the internet, colleges and also high school counseling offices to gather information.
3. Attend college nights and participate in pre-college programs if available.
4. Apply to several colleges and visit at least 1 year prior to your attending.
5. Complete your applications by answering all questions with neat handwriting or online.
6. Provide supportive data such as letters of recommendations or essays.

Selecting and Applying to a College affirmations

I will do the research necessary to ensure that I select the college that is best for me. I will spend time on the internet and research at least five colleges and plan to visit at least three of these colleges. I will speak with my counselor at school and any other mentor that will help me get the desired information. This helps me select the college that best meets my needs. I must apply to several colleges at least one year to a semester before I plan to attend. I will complete several applications either online or by paper application. I will get the application fees, transcripts, essays and any other paperwork required to complete my application packet information. I will follow-up to be sure all my information has been received if I have not heard from the college in an appropriate time frame. I will be sure to take the appropriate college entrance exams ahead of time so that I meet all deadlines. My applications will be neat and reflect my attention to detail and excellence. I will get at least two recommendation letters and submit an autobiographical essay. I am confident I will be accepted at several colleges because I am prepared academically, organizationally and socially.

Write your own Selecting and Applying to College affirmation/goals

_____

_____

_____

_____

_____

_____

_____

_____

_____

_____

_____

_____

Chapter 13: Financial Aid and Scholarships

Keep the charge of the Lord your God, walk in His ways, keep His statutes, His commandments, His precepts, and His testimonies, as it is written in the Law of Moses, that you may do wisely and prosper in all that you do and wherever you turn according to 1 Kings 2:3.

One of the most important steps next to selecting your college is obtaining financial aid or scholarships. The cost for college has continued to increase and can range from $500 a year to $50,000 or more depending upon if you are a full-time or part-time student. Also highly selective and private colleges tend to cost more than public universities. Some parents have saved money through a variety of college savings plans, however, very few students are set up to cover all of their college costs completely.

As a prospective student, you should research the cost of the university you are considering at the same time you are narrowing down your top college choices. The cost of the college can be a determining factor in your ability to attend or not. If you are considering a $45,000 a year college, yet you have no option for financial aid, scholarship or family contribution, you may need to select another college until your finances line up with the expected college expenses. However, you may be able to afford your college of choice if you research ahead of time and have other scholarship options and family contributions available to you.

Colleges expect you to pay all the expenses that are needed to attend. All financial costs are provided to you in a variety of literature so you must make sure you are in a position to pay. Stress will definitely set in if you find yourself unable to cover your college expenses. Financial aid information brochures are available from most colleges and are available to help describe the college financial aid process. Typically these brochures include information about scholarships, tuition and room and board costs. Financial aid is usually based upon family incomes and W2's while scholarship qualifications vary based on academic levels, test scores, athletic ability or academic interests.

Many scholarships will require that you complete an application while some are granted if you meet a specific criteria outlined in the financial aid brochures or a website. My college expenses were covered from an array of areas for each degree. The Spelman College experience was a great opportunity for me. The cost did not ever enter my mind, however, I was almost certain that it would be difficult for me to attend. My mother was single and it appeared that it would be a great strain on her finances. However, she pulled it off and cashed in some stocks and that coupled with financial aid made my Spelman opportunity possible. Sometimes we have to be selfish when it comes to our college choice, however, we need to be sure that our family, need based or scholarship monies are an accessible option for us to consider.

After a year and a half at Spelman, I transferred to Western Michigan University. Fortunately the cost was lower and my financial aid transferred without a problem. Work study jobs were also available to me and these opportunities allowed me to work on campus and earn spending money while attending college. Most college career centers will post available internships, college work study and off campus jobs for those that are interested or eligible.

I pursued my master's degree four years after obtaining my bachelor's degree. My master's degree was primarily paid for through tuition reimbursement offered through my employer. Tuition reimbursement is an excellent option for those that need support for college. You simply pay the money up front in some cases and submit the receipts to your employer. Some employers pay a percentage while others may pay 100% of the tuition. On most occasions I would charge my classes and pay my credit card back after reimbursement. It may be best for some of you to pursue employers that provide tuition reimbursement especially if you are considering additional college and are low on funds.

Finally, at the doctoral level, I was blessed to obtain two fellowships that paid for all of my doctoral studies. Through my previous employer I received a $20,000 King Chavez Parks Fellowship. My current employer also contributed $10,000 through this same program to assist with the remaining expenses that were incurred for course work. There are many fellowships available; however, you will have to spend time searching for funding through networking, on the internet, in books or through search services that provide this type of information.

Practical applications for Financial Aid and Scholarships

1. Research scholarship and financial aid information.
2. Request financial aid information from your college of choice.
3. Speak with your counselor or career center about scholarship opportunities.
4. Discuss your college expenses with your family to determine what your family can afford.
5. Complete the Free application for federal student aid. (FAFSA)

Financial Aid and Scholarship Affirmations

I can afford my college of choice. There is enough money out there to support me and my college expenses. I will not let the cost of college deter me or stop me from completing applications to the colleges that offer my programs. My skills and talents are going to be a great contribution to my college of choice. I can work on campus or get a job in my college community if I have a need for extra money. I am going to complete the FAFSA in a timely manner to ensure that I get the most financial aid possible. I will attract all the support I need to attend the college of my choice. I will have all the scholarship, financial aid and family support necessary to complete my education. I will always stay in school and work beyond my obstacles so that I can complete my college education.

Write your own Financial affirmation/goals

_____

_____

_____

_____

_____

_____

_____

_____

_____

_____

_____

_____

Chapter 14: Selecting a Major

Jeremiah 29:11 says For I know the thoughts and plans that I have for you, says the Lord, thoughts and plans for welfare and peace and not for evil, to give you hope in your final outcome.

Selecting a major for college can be difficult and requires great contemplation. Your major should reflect some area that is of interest to you. Many freshman students that are about to enter college are specific about their major while others have three to eight areas of interest. Liberal Arts colleges are typically designed to provide you with a two year general education curriculum to help broaden your understanding of the world, people and other academic areas.

Some course work for particular majors may not be

available to you until you complete some general education courses, prerequisite courses or apply to get into the specific program. Prerequisite courses are classes that help prepare you for the courses offered in your major area. If you are undecided about your major, you can start to ask yourself a series of questions. For instance:

1. Do I like working with people?

2. Do I like numbers?

3. Do I enjoy research?

4. Does the world of technology excite me?

5. Do I want to make a lot of money?

6. Am I more into helping people with their problems?

7. Do I like working with my hands?

8.   Am I creative?

9.   Would I consider myself a leader or a follower?

10.   What am I passionate about?

The above questions are designed to get you thinking about what you like and what you don't like. There are also many career and personality inventories that can help you assess areas that best fit your future opportunities. Inventories help explore your interests by asking you a series of questions that produce an assortment of career options that best reveal your response to the questions. You can also wait to select your major after you begin college and take a few classes. There are some majors that require prerequisite courses while others chart out the plan of courses you should take for the entire time you are in college.

You will want to investigate your majors to be sure that you have an idea of what is required of you. The college catalog and major course descriptions can also help you decide what major is best for you. You can read up on all the classes that are offered in your field and assess whether or not the classes are of interest to you. It is also important to participate in internships and perform volunteer work in areas that you are considering. This is a way for you to rule out careers that don't reflect your strengths. Please note that in many cases some people major in a field and then work in another field that is totally unrelated to their major.

There are also many careers that are not a major but exist as an occupational choice. A college admissions officer is one such area and there are many others. It is important that you gain the skill set needed to enhance your strengths and minimize your weaknesses. This will allow you to qualify for opportunities and stand above your competitors. I selected a Psychology major in undergraduate school based on my desire to help others. My dream was to be a Psychologist and counsel people whenever and wherever there was a need. However, after graduation I was not interested in that field at all. This major still gave me opportunities to work as a Child Care Associate Director, personal banker, flight attendant and counselor for several non profit organizations.

Four years later, I pursued my master's degree in Public Administration. This was not an easy decision. I was considering law school, business school and psychology. I requested materials from several graduate schools. I took the GMAT (the business school entrance test) the GRE (the liberal studies graduate school entrance test) and I sat in on a class about the LSAT (the law school entrance exam). My outcome resulted in attendance at Wayne State University's Public Administration program. My GRE score wasn't that great, however, I was on to something. My new dream was to help cities and be part of making a difference for others through the city's administration system. I was going to be a public administrator. That dream did not last long, although I finished my master's degree. It was determined after working at a City Hall that politics were not suited for me. It did not fit my personality and it definitely did not excite me. The information gained was beneficial to me although my public administration degree was not realized in a city setting.

Ten years later, my dream of getting my doctoral degree became a reality. Believe it or not, I went through the same process as with my master's degree pursuit. However, I was certain education was the area for me. It was more practical for me this time when making my choice. The school had to be close because I had a family; the program had to be of interest to me because I had to produce a dissertation. I began thinking about my topic for the dissertation before entering the doctoral program. This was an important decision as research for my classes included the gathering of initial data that would help me gain more knowledge about my topic. The most important aspect needed to select your major is to know yourself and to know what interest you the most. My doctoral study was on the Amistad Academy, an after school program in Flint, MI that was founded by mother through Career Alliance. I benefited immensely from after school programs while my mother was working, so this was the best choice of study for me.

Your interests may change over time and that is a natural part of life. However, you can save time on switching majors if you spend time working, researching or volunteering in several arenas before your actual schooling begins. Please note that it is a normal occurrence to change a major at some point during the educational process.

Practical applications for Selecting a Major:

1. Research different career paths
2. Meet with career counselors and advisors
3. Take an inventory test to determine career interests
4. Volunteer, work or intern to learn new skills

Selecting a Major affirmation:

I am confident that my purpose will be revealed to me. I was born to perform a specific function in excellence. My career choice will be fun and I will enjoy what I do every day. I know as I experience new things, people and places I will move closer to the field of work I was born to perform. My eyes, ears and heart will be open to new ideas. I am willing to volunteer, intern and serve in areas that will help me narrow down my career choice. The right people and advisors will be directed to me and I do not have to be concerned or confused about my life's work. I will perform my very best in whatever I put my hands, heart and mind to and I will be a joy to be around. I will love the career that I select. I understand that I may change careers and if that occurs, God will give me the grace, wisdom and understanding to know when it is time to move on to another career path. My training will be continuous as I know that I want to understand all the latest ideas and technology that are occurring in my field.

Write your own Selecting a Major affirmation/goals

_____

_____

_____

_____

_____

_____

_____

_____

_____

_____

_____

_____

_____

Chapter 15: Moving Past Discouragement

You will show me the path of life; in Your presence is fullness of joy, at Your right hand, there are pleasures forevermore according to Psalms 16:11.

Discouragement can set in while you are pursuing your college education. I have met many people that stop college for a variety of reasons. Perhaps you run out of money or you have a relationship challenge or break-up, or maybe there are deaths in the family. You may even lose your job or you, your child or family member becomes ill. Whatever the case may be, you can still complete your education and stay on track to meet your dream of completing your college education.

You could even be overwhelmed with the course work and the challenge that arises when trying to balance everything in your life. As I mentioned earlier, I became discouraged while I was near the end of my doctoral program. They indicated there was a problem with some of my classes and it would need to be straightened out before my program could be completed.

This was a major concern since 4 ½ years of schooling, including several major exams and my dissertation had been completed. I began praying and moving forward with the goal of completion in mind. And David was greatly distressed according to 1 Samuel 30:6; but David encouraged himself in the Lord his God. I also had to encourage myself.

All the appropriate telephone calls were made. Classmates, friends, my parents, professors, college administrators and many others were contacted. I began looking through all my paperwork to ensure everything was in order.

Finally, I reached the person that could help get everything straightened out. He was a kind man and not only did he straighten everything out, but he comforted me as well and told me everything was going to be alright. He was my personal angel.

First Corinthians 1:4 says Who comforts us in all our tribulation, that we may be able to comfort them which are in any trouble, by the comfort wherewith we ourselves are comforted of God. In the midst of the uncertainty, I still proceeded as if everything was going to work out fine. The notification of approval came the day before I defended my dissertation and everything worked out perfect and in order.

You will get discouraged, it may even look like things will not work out, however, in the midst of this, you must move forward. Hebrews 11:1 reminds me that faith is the substance of things hoped for, the evidence of things not seen. You have to keep moving ahead even if you don't know the outcome, even if you don't have the money and even if you don't think you can make it another day. Our victory comes in our moving forward in spite of our circumstances. Keep moving forward and the completion of your degree will be eminent and evident for all to see. You can do it!!!

<u>Practical applications for Moving Past Discouragement</u>

1. Stay in communication with supportive family members
2. Stay in communication with your professors
3. Make sure you are prepared for each class
4. Balance your time and your schedule

Moving Past Discouragement affirmations

I can overcome any obstacle that comes my way. Even though I may get discouraged about my grades, my finances or my family life, I can still be victorious and complete my education. I can keep moving forward by taking the classes I need and by getting help in courses that are difficult for me. I will develop my mind during this time while I am in school and learn all that is available to me. I will make extra effort to take good notes and get to class on time. I will organize my time and balance my family life ahead of time so that I can complete all assignments. I will be responsible and accountable to my class, my job and my family so that I feel good about myself and my experiences.

Write your own Moving Past Discouragement

affirmation/goals

_____

_____

_____

_____

_____

_____

_____

_____

_____

_____

_____

_____

LaVergne, TN USA
05 January 2010
168949LV00002B/3/P